Table of Contents

INTRODUCTION	2
CHAPTER 1: INTRODUCTION TO ENTREPRENEURSHIP	5
CHAPTER 2: DEVELOPING A BUSINESS IDEA	8
CHAPTER 3: MARKET RESEARCH AND CUSTOMER DISCOVERY	12
CHAPTER 4: CRAFTING A BUSINESS PLAN	16
CHAPTER 5: UNDERSTANDING BUSINESS MODELS	20
CHAPTER 6: FUNDING YOUR BUSINESS	24
CHAPTER 7: BUILDING A BRAND	28
CHAPTER 8: MARKETING AND SALES FUNDAMENTALS	32
CHAPTER 9: OPERATIONS AND MANAGEMENT BASICS	36
CHAPTER 10: BUILDING AND MANAGING A TEAM	40
CHAPTER 11: FINANCIAL BASICS FOR ENTREPRENEURS	44
CHAPTER 12: LEGAL AND REGULATORY BASICS	48
CHAPTER 13: RISK MANAGEMENT AND PROBLEM SOLVING	52
CHAPTER 14: SCALING AND GROWING THE BUSINESS	56
CHAPTER 15: EXIT STRATEGIES AND FUTURE PLANNING	60

CHAPTER 16: ENTREPRENEURIAL MINDSET AND CONTINUOUS LEARNING 66

CONCLUSION 70

Introduction

Entrepreneurship Basics Q&A, is for anyone who wants to start or improve their business. It gives clear, practical advice on important topics like finding a business idea, planning, marketing, managing money, and growing your company. Each chapter is written in a simple question-and-answer style to help you easily understand and use the ideas.

Entrepreneurship is about creating something valuable, solving problems, and following your own path. It's exciting but also challenging. This book is your guide to handle those challenges and take steps toward success.

Whether you're new to business, running a small company, or turning your skills into a business, this book has something for you. You can read it all or focus on the sections that matter most to you right now. It's filled with tips and strategies you can start using right away.

Starting a business takes effort and courage, but it's a journey worth taking. This book will help you every step of the way, so you can build something meaningful. Let's get started!

Entrepreneurship Basics Q&A

by

Pinnacle Press

ENTREPRENEURSHIP
BASICS

Q&A

PINNACLE PRESS

Chapter 1: Introduction to Entrepreneurship

1. What is entrepreneurship?

Entrepreneurship means starting and running a new business to make money or bring new ideas to the market.

2. Who can be an entrepreneur?

Anyone who is passionate, ready to take risks, and wants to solve problems can be an entrepreneur.

3. Why do people start businesses?

People start businesses to earn money, follow their passion, solve problems, or have more freedom.

4. Are there myths about entrepreneurship?

Yes, some common myths are:

Entrepreneurs are born, not made.
Only young people can start businesses.
You need a lot of money to begin.
It's a quick way to get rich.

5. What are the good and hard parts of being an entrepreneur?

Good: Freedom, flexibility, and personal satisfaction.
Hard: Uncertainty, financial risks, and long working hours.

6. How do I know if I'm ready to start a business?

You might be ready if:

You're motivated by more than money.
You can handle stress and challenges.
You're willing to work hard and learn.

7. How is entrepreneurship different from a regular job?

Regular jobs often give stability and set work hours. Entrepreneurship involves risks, flexible hours, and full responsibility for the business.

8. What types of entrepreneurs are there?

Small business owners.
Start-up founders.
Social entrepreneurs solving problems.
People innovating inside big companies.
Lifestyle entrepreneurs who follow their passions.

9. Is it better to start alone or with a partner?

It depends:

Alone: Full control but more pressure.
With a partner: Shared work but needs trust and clear communication.

10. What steps should I take to start?

Identify a problem or passion.
Research the market and customers.
Write down your goals and ideas.
Test your idea on a small scale.

11. Why is passion important?

Passion keeps you motivated during tough times and helps you stay focused.

12. How important is creativity?

Creativity helps you find new ideas and stand out, but it must work with good planning.

13. Can entrepreneurship be learned?

Yes, you can learn entrepreneurship through experience, education, and practice.

Chapter 2: Developing a Business Idea

1. How do I come up with a business idea?

To come up with a business idea, look for problems you care about solving or things that could be improved. Talk to people, research what's missing in the market, and keep an open mind to spot opportunities.

2. What types of business ideas are there?

Products: Selling items like clothes or gadgets.
Services: Offering skills, like tutoring or cleaning.
Tech: Creating apps or software.
Platforms: Building a marketplace, like online shops.
Subscriptions: Providing regular services, like meal kits.

3. How do I know if my idea is original or good for the market?

To know if your idea is original or good for the market, research what's already out there. Find gaps or ways to make things better, cheaper, or faster. Check if people want the product and will pay for it.

4. What's the difference between creating something new and improving an idea?

Creating something new brings fresh solutions. Improving an idea means tweaking what already exists. Both can succeed if done well.

5. How do I test my business idea?

To test your business idea:

Talk to potential customers.
Create a simple version of your product.

Run small tests to see if people are interested.
Try pre-sales or crowdfunding to check demand.

6. Where can I find ideas for businesses?

To find ideas for businesses:

Solve problems you've faced.
Listen to what people need.
Watch market trends or new tech.
Study competitors and their weaknesses.
Turn your hobbies into a business.

7. How do I find a real problem to solve?

To find a real problem to solve, listen for complaints or frustrations people have. Use surveys or interviews to confirm that the problem is common and worth solving.

8. What is a USP, and why does it matter?

A USP (unique selling point) is what makes your business different. Find out what makes your product better, faster, or easier to use than others.

9. Should I target a small group or a big audience?

Start with a small group (niche) to focus your efforts and grow from there. Broad audiences need more resources to reach.

10. What is a "pain point" in business?

A pain point is a problem or frustration people have. Solving pain points creates demand because people are eager to fix them.

11. How important is timing and trends?

Timing matters. Starting a business during a rising trend or growing need can help it succeed faster.

12. How can I find groups or markets that are being ignored?

To find groups or markets that are being ignored, look for gaps in existing products, underserved communities, or trends that competitors haven't noticed.

13. How do I pick between several ideas?

To pick between several ideas, consider these:

Which idea has the most demand?
Which one excites you the most?
Which is easiest to start with your skills and budget?

14. What is an MVP, and why is it useful?

An MVP (minimum viable product) is a simple version of your product to test the idea. It helps you get feedback without spending too much time or money.

15. How can I tell if my idea can grow?

To tell if your idea can grow, check if you can reach more customers easily, use tech to save time, or expand to other locations or products.

16. Should I think about international markets?

If your idea works globally, it's worth considering. Test it locally first to make sure it's successful.

17. Why is customer feedback important?

Customers can tell you what they need and what to improve. Their feedback saves time and helps you make better decisions.

18. What if my idea isn't new?

If your idea isn't new, focus on doing it better. Improve quality, lower costs, or offer something competitors don't. Execution can be more important than originality.

Chapter 3: Market Research and Customer Discovery

1. Why is market research important?

Marketing research helps you understand your customers, find demand for your product, and know your competition. This reduces risks and helps you make better decisions.

2. What's the difference between primary and secondary research?

Primary: You collect new data (surveys, interviews).
Secondary: You use existing data (reports, studies).

3. How do I find my target audience

To find your target audience, think about who will use your product. Look at their age, location, income, and interests. Create profiles of your ideal customers.

4. What is a customer persona?

A customer persona is a made-up profile of your perfect customer, showing their needs, habits, and goals. It helps you focus your product and marketing.

5. What are ways to do market research?

Ways to do market research include:

Surveys: Ask people questions.
Interviews: Talk to customers in detail.
Focus groups: Small discussions with potential customers.
Social listening: Watch online conversations.

6. How can I understand my customers?

Ask them directly through surveys or interviews. Check reviews of similar products to see what people like or dislike.

7. What is competitor analysis?

Competitor analysis is studying your competitors to learn their strengths, weaknesses, and strategies. It helps you stand out and find gaps in the market.

8. How do I do a competitor analysis?

Look at competitors' prices, reviews, marketing, and products. Use tools like SWOT (Strengths, Weaknesses, Opportunities, Threats).

9. What are cheap ways to do market research?

Cheap ways to do market research include:

Using free tools like Google Forms for surveys.
Watching discussions on Reddit or social media.
Analyzing competitors' customer reviews.

10. How do I find the size of my target market?

To find the size of your target market, estimate how many people might buy your product using industry reports and online data.

11. Why use surveys?

Surveys give you direct feedback from potential customers about their needs, interests, and price preferences.

12. How do focus groups help?

Focus groups let you hear detailed opinions about your idea from a small group of target customers.

13. What is social listening?

Social listening is watching online discussions about your industry, product, or competitors to understand trends and opinions.

14. How do I check if people want my product?

To check if people want your product:

Test with a simple product.
Run pre-sales or crowdfunding.
See online searches for related topics.

15. How do I use customer feedback?

To use customer feedback:

Fix problems customers mention, improve features they like, and use their suggestions to grow your business.

16. What's the difference between quantitative and qualitative research?

Quantitative: Numbers and facts (e.g., surveys).
Qualitative: Opinions and feelings (e.g., interviews).

17. How should I handle bad feedback?

To handle bad feedback, listen carefully and ask questions to understand. Use it to improve your product.

18. Should market research be ongoing?

Yes, customer needs and trends change. Keep asking for feedback and watching the market.

19. How do I analyze my research data?

To analyze research data, group similar feedback, look for patterns, and create charts to make the data easier to understand.

20. How does market research help with my value proposition?

Market research shows what customers need and what competitors lack. Use this to explain why your product is the best choice.

Chapter 4: Crafting a Business Plan

1. What is a business plan, and why do I need one?

A business plan is a document that explains your business goals, market, strategy, and finances. It helps you stay organized, attract investors, and guide your business.

2. What are the main parts of a business plan?

The main parts of a business plan are:

Executive Summary: Overview of the business.
Company Description: What your business does.
Market Analysis: Research on the industry and competitors.
Organization and Management: Details about your team.
Product/Service Description: What you're offering.
Marketing and Sales Plan: How you'll reach customers.
Financial Plan: Budgets and profit estimates.

3. What is an executive summary?

An executive summary is a short introduction to your business idea, goals, and why it will succeed. It's usually one page and grabs the reader's attention.

4. What goes in the company description?

Information about your mission, goals, business structure (like LLC or corporation), and what makes your business unique.

5. How do I do a market analysis?

To do a market analysis, research your industry, target customers, and competitors. Include trends, customer needs, and gaps in the market that you can fill.

6. What is included in the "Organization and Management" section?

The Organization and Management section show how your business is structured and who is on your team. Include roles, experience, and ownership details.

7. How do I describe my product or service?

To describe your product or service, explain what it does, how it helps customers, and what makes it different from competitors.

8. What is a unique value proposition (UVP)?

A unique value proposition (UVP) is what makes your business special and why customers should choose you over others.

9. How do I create a marketing and sales plan?

To create a marketing and sales plan, describe how you'll find customers (social media, ads, etc.), how you'll sell to them, and how you'll keep them coming back.

10. What is a funding request?

A funding request is a section that explains how much money you need, what you'll use it for, and how you'll pay it back (if it's a loan).

11. How do I make financial projections?

To make financial projections, include estimates for revenue, costs, and profits. Use data from market research to make realistic predictions.

12. What is a break-even analysis?

A break-even analysis shows when your sales will cover your costs, helping you understand when your business might start making a profit.

13. How can I show profitability?

To show profitability, include revenue forecasts, cost breakdowns, and profit margins backed by research.

14. What should I put in the appendix?

Put supporting documents like resumes, product images, legal agreements, or market data in the appendix.

15. How long should a business plan be?

A business plan should be typically 15-30 pages, but it depends on your business. Focus on being clear and concise.

16. How often should I update my business plan?

Review it yearly or whenever there's a big change in your business, like new goals or funding.

17. How do I make my business plan stand out?

Keep the business plan clear, include solid market research, realistic financials, and highlight what makes your business unique.

18. What mistakes should I avoid?

Here are mistakes you should avoid:

Don't overestimate revenue or underestimate costs.
Don't ignore competitors.
Don't be vague about your target audience.
Don't skip market research.

19. Should I hire a professional to help?

You can write it yourself, but a professional can help with complex parts like finances or refining the plan for investors.

20. How do I use my business plan?

Use your business plan to guide your decisions, track your progress, and share with investors or partners. Keep it updated as your business grows.

Chapter 5: Understanding Business Models

1. What is a business model?

A business model is a plan for how your business makes money, delivers value to customers, and runs its operations.

2. Why is a business model important?

A business model is important because it helps you define how to attract customers, earn profits, and manage resources effectively.

3. What types of business models are there?

Here are the types of business models:

Direct Sales: Selling directly to customers.
Subscription: Charging customers regularly.
Freemium: Free basic service with paid premium options.
E-commerce: Selling products online.
Marketplace: Connecting buyers and sellers.
Licensing: Charging others to use your intellectual property.
Franchise: Selling the rights to use your brand and model.

4. How do I choose the best business model?

To choose the best business model, think about your product, audience, and industry. Test small versions of your model and learn from successful businesses in your field.

5. What is a value proposition?

A value proposition is what makes your product special and why customers should pick you over others.

6. How do I create a unique value proposition (UVP)?

To create a UVP, focus on the main benefit your product provides and what makes it different. Test it with customers to see if it works.

7. What is the Lean Business Model Canvas?

The Lean Business Model Canvas is a simple, one-page way to outline your business, covering customers, value, revenue, costs, and key activities.

8. What is scalability, and why does it matter?

Scalability is about growing your business without big cost increases. It's important for long-term growth.

9. How do I ensure my business model is sustainable?

To ensure your business model is sustainable, build strong customer relationships, control costs, and adapt to market changes.

10. What is a pivot, and when should I do it?

A pivot is a big change to your business model when it's not working. Do it if you see better opportunities or need to fix major issues.

11. Can I mix different business models?

Yes, combining models like e-commerce and subscriptions can increase revenue but must be managed carefully.

12. How do I build strong partnerships?

To build strong partnerships, work with suppliers, distributors, or other businesses that complement your strengths and help expand your reach.

13. What are revenue streams, and how can I diversify them?

Revenue streams are ways you make money. You can add more by offering new products, upgrades, or licensing.

14. How do I create a subscription-based model?

To create a subscription-based model, offer something customers need often, set clear pricing, and focus on keeping them satisfied.

15. What is a freemium model work?

A freemium model offers a free version of your product to attract users, then charge for extra features.

16. How does an e-commerce model work?

An e-commerce model sells products online through a website or platform. Focus on good marketing, inventory management, and customer service.

17. What is a licensing model?

A licensing model is when you let others use your intellectual property in exchange for fees or royalties.

18. How do I know if my business model is financially viable?

To know if your business model is financially viable, check if your revenue will be greater than your costs over time. Use tools like break-even analysis.

19. How do I test my business model?

Start with a small-scale launch or MVP to see if customers like your product and if the model works.

20. What are examples of great business models?

Apple: Combines product sales with subscriptions.
Amazon: E-commerce, subscriptions, and cloud services.
Netflix: Subscription model with unique content.
Tesla: Direct sales with innovative products.

These examples can inspire you to find what works for your business.

Chapter 6: Funding Your Business

1. Why do I need funding for my business?

Funding helps cover startup costs, grow your business, and reduce financial stress so you can focus on success.

2. What are the main types of funding?

Bootstrapping: Using personal savings or revenue.
Friends and Family: Borrowing from people you know.
Loans: Borrowed money with interest.
Grants: Free money you don't repay.
Angel Investors: Individuals investing in exchange for equity.
Venture Capital: Firms investing for a share of ownership.
Crowdfunding: Raising small amounts from many people online.

3. How do I choose between bootstrapping and external funding?

Bootstrapping gives you control but limits growth speed. External funding offers faster growth but often requires sharing ownership or repaying loans.

4. What is bootstrapping?

Bootstrapping is using your own money or business profits to grow. It gives you control and teaches disciplined spending.

5. How do I raise money from friends and family?

To raise money from friends and family, present your idea professionally, set clear terms, and be honest about risks to maintain trust.

6. What are business loans?

Business loans is money borrowed from banks or lenders that you repay over time with interest. They're useful for growth if you can repay.

7. What is an SBA loan?

An SBA loan is a government-backed loan with lower rates and better terms for small businesses. You need a solid plan and good credit to qualify.

8. What are grants?

Grants are free funding from governments or organizations, often for specific industries or purposes. Check eligibility and apply carefully.

9. What is angel investing?

Angel investing is when individuals invest money in early-stage businesses for equity or convertible debt, often offering guidance too.

10. How do I attract angel investors?

To attract angel investors, have a strong pitch, show early success or customer interest, and network through events or platforms like AngelList.

11. What is venture capital (VC)?

VC is when firms invest in high-growth businesses for equity. Seek VC if you need large amounts of capital and are ready to scale.

12. How do I prepare for a VC pitch?

To prepare for a VC pitch, make a clear pitch deck, show traction, and practice your presentation to highlight your team, market, and potential.

13. What is crowdfunding?

Crowdfunding is raising money online from many small investors or backers. It's great for ideas with mass appeal.

14. How do I run a successful crowdfunding campaign?

To run a successful crowdfunding campaign, create a compelling story, use visuals, set realistic goals, and promote on social media to engage supporters.

15. What is equity crowdfunding?

Equity crowdfunding is when people invest in your business for ownership shares instead of rewards. It's good for raising larger sums.

16. How do I decide how much funding I need?

To decide how much funding you need, add up startup costs, monthly expenses, and growth needs. Be realistic and include a safety buffer.

17. What are the risks of giving up equity?

The risks of giving up equity are:

Loss of control: Investors may influence decisions.
Dilution: Future funding reduces your ownership.
Pressure: Investors expect returns quickly.

18. What are convertible notes?

Convertible notes are loans that turn into equity during future funding rounds. Useful for early funding without setting a valuation.

19. What is a SAFE agreement?

A Simple Agreement for Future Equity gives investors equity later, like convertible notes, but without interest or maturity dates.

20. How can I improve my chances of getting funding?

To improve your chances of getting funding:

Create a solid business plan.
Show early success or customer interest.
Build a strong team.
Network and pitch confidently.

Be ready to answer tough questions.
Persistence and preparation are key to finding the right funding for your business.

Chapter 7: Building a Brand

1. What is a brand, and why is it important?

A brand is your business's identity, including values, image, and messaging. It helps build trust, stand out from competitors, and keep customers loyal.

2. How do I define my brand identity?

To define your brand identity, think about your business's mission, values, and what makes it unique. Make sure your brand identity reflects this in everything you do, from your logo to customer service.

3. What are the key elements of a brand?

The key elements of a brand identity are:

Logo: Your business's visual symbol.
Colors: Reflect your brand's personality.
Typography: Fonts that match your tone.
Tagline: A memorable phrase about your brand.
Voice: How you communicate.
Story: Your company's purpose and journey.

4. What is a brand story, and how do I create one?

A brand story is the story of why your business exists, the challenges you've faced, and your vision. Make it authentic and relatable to connect emotionally with customers.

5. How do I define my target audience?

To define your target audience, identify who is most likely to buy from you by considering their age, lifestyle, location, and what problems your product solves.

6. What role does a logo play?

A logo is a key part of your brand. It should be simple, memorable, and reflect your business's personality.

7. How do I choose the right colors?

To choose the right colors, pick colors that match your brand's mood and appeal to your audience. For example:

Blue: Trust.
Red: Energy.
Green: Growth.

8. What is brand voice, and how do I create it?

Brand voice is how your business "sounds." Decide if your tone is friendly, professional, or quirky, and stay consistent across all communications.

9. How do I create a memorable tagline?

To create a memorable tagline, make it short, catchy, and focused on what makes your business special.

10. What is brand positioning, and why does it matter?

Brand positioning is how your brand stands out from competitors. It tells customers why they should choose you.

11. What is a brand style guide, and why do I need one?

A brand style guide keeps your branding consistent. Include logo rules, colors, fonts, voice, and preferred imagery.

12. What are cost-effective ways to build brand awareness?

Cost-effective ways to build brand awareness include:

Using social media.
Writing blogs or create videos.
Partnering with other brands.
Encouraging referrals from happy customers.

13. How can social media strengthen my brand?

You can use social media to share stories, engage with customers, and show your brand's personality with consistent visuals and tone.

14. How does customer experience affect branding?

Positive customer experiences build trust and loyalty. Every interaction, from your website to customer support, should reflect your brand values.

15. How do I keep brand consistency as I grow?

To keep brand consistency as you grow, train your team on brand guidelines and check that all messaging and visuals stay aligned with your identity.

16. Why is storytelling important for branding?

Storytelling makes your brand relatable and memorable. Share your journey, customer successes, or behind-the-scenes moments.

17. What is brand loyalty, and how do I build it?

Brand loyalty means customers keep choosing you. Build it with quality products, great service, and rewards for repeat customers.

18. How do I handle negative feedback?

To handle negative feedback, listen, empathize, and offer solutions. Handling criticism well shows you care about customers and protects your reputation.

19. How can I measure my brand's success?

To measure brand's success, track metrics like:

Awareness (mentions, traffic).
Loyalty (repeat purchases).
Engagement (likes, shares).
Customer satisfaction (surveys).

20. How do I keep my brand relevant?

To keep your brand relevant, stay updated on trends, refresh your visuals, adapt your messaging, and listen to customer feedback to stay connected to your audience.

Chapter 8: Marketing and Sales Fundamentals

1. What's the difference between marketing and sales?

Marketing creates interest and awareness about your business, while sales focuses on converting that interest into paying customers.

2. How do I create a marketing plan?

To create a marketing plan:

Define your target audience.
Set clear goals.
Pick marketing channels like social media or email.
Create a budget and timeline.

3. What is a target market, and why is it important?

A target market is the group most likely to buy your product. Knowing your target market helps you focus your efforts and messaging for better results.

4. How do I choose the best marketing channels?

Find out where your audience spends time. Use social media, email, SEO, or other channels based on your audience's habits and preferences.

5. What is digital marketing, and how can it help?

Digital marketing includes all online strategies like social media and email. It's cost-effective, measurable, and helps you reach a broad audience.

6. What are the basics of social media marketing?

The basics of social media marketing are:

Picking platforms your audience uses.
Posting valuable content regularly.
Using visuals and interact with your followers.

7. How does content marketing work?

Content marketing builds trust by providing helpful, engaging content like blogs or videos. It attracts your audience and positions your brand as an expert.

8. What is email marketing, and how do I start?

Email marketing involves sending updates and offers to subscribers. Start by collecting email addresses and sending regular, relevant content.

9. What is SEO, and why does it matter?

SEO (Search Engine Optimization) helps your website rank higher in search results, increasing visibility and organic traffic.

10. How do I develop a sales strategy?

To develop a sales strategy, you need to:

Understand your customers' needs.
Pick sales channels.
Set realistic goals and track results.
Train your team on selling techniques.

11. What is the sales funnel?

The sales funnel guides customers from learning about your brand to making a purchase. Key stages: awareness, interest, decision, and action.

12. How can I generate leads?

To generate leads, use strategies like content marketing, social media ads, free resources, or networking to attract potential customers.

13. How do I convert leads into customers?

To convert leads into customers, build trust, show your product's value, and follow up with personalized messages or offers.

14. What is customer retention, and why is it important?

Customer retention is about keeping customers loyal. Loyal customers are easier and cheaper to keep and often spend more over time.

15. How do I create a loyalty program?

To create a loyalty program, reward repeat purchases with discounts, points, or special perks. Make it simple and appealing for customers to join.

16. What are KPIs, and why do they matter?

KPIs (Key Performance Indicators) measure success. Examples include customer acquisition cost, conversion rate, and retention rate.

17. How do I set and track a marketing budget?

To set and track a marketing budget, allocate funds based on your revenue and goals. Track spending and measure results to see which channels give the best return.

18. How do I create a value proposition for sales?

To create a value proposition for sales, highlight the unique benefits of your product, focusing on how it solves customer problems.

19. How does customer feedback help?

Customer feedback shows what customers like or want improved. Use it to refine your marketing, products, and sales strategies.

20. How do I adapt to changing trends?

To adapt to changing trends:

Monitor industry trends and customer needs. Experiment with new ideas, adjust messaging, and stay flexible to remain competitive.

Chapter 9: Operations and Management Basics

1. What are the essential operations for a new business?

Core tasks like delivering products or services, managing inventory, handling customer service, monitoring finances, and driving sales and marketing.

2. How do I set up efficient processes and workflows?

To set up efficient processes and workflows:

Map out each step, find and fix bottlenecks, and document processes. Use tools or automation to save time and improve efficiency.

3. What is inventory management, and why is it important?

Inventory management is about tracking stock levels to avoid running out or overstocking. Good inventory management saves money and keeps customers happy.

4. What are the basics of supply chain management?

The basics of supply chain management are:

Managing suppliers, logistics, and product quality. A strong supply chain reduces costs and avoids delays.

5. How do I manage day-to-day operations as a solo entrepreneur?

Focus on priorities, use tools to stay organized, and outsource tasks like accounting or design when needed.

6. What is the role of technology in managing operations?

Technology helps streamline tasks, improve accuracy, and boost productivity with tools for project management, inventory tracking, customer relationships, and accounting.

7. How do I choose the right tools for my business?

To choose the right tools for your business:

Identify your needs, research options, and test tools with free trials. Pick ones that are user-friendly, scalable, and cost-effective.

8. What is quality control, and how do I implement it?

Quality control is ensuring products or services meet standards. Set clear expectations, inspect regularly, and use customer feedback to improve.

9. How can I effectively manage customer service?

To effectively manage customer service:

Respond quickly, handle issues with empathy, and collect feedback to improve. Use tools like chat or email to stay organized.

10. How do I handle complaints and negative feedback?

To handle complaints and negative feedback:

Listen, empathize, and resolve issues quickly. Learn from complaints to prevent future problems.

11. What is cash flow management, and why is it important?

Cash flow management is tracking money in and out of your business. Positive cash flow ensures you can pay expenses, grow, and handle surprises.

12. How do I manage my business's finances?

To manage your business finances, track income and expenses, set a budget, and review financial statements regularly. Use accounting software to simplify this.

13. What is the role of budgeting in operations management?

Budgeting helps control spending and allocate resources. Monitor expenses monthly and adjust as needed.

14. How do I hire and train employees?

To hire and train employees:

Define roles clearly, hire people with matching skills, and create onboarding materials. Provide regular feedback and growth opportunities.

15. How do I motivate and retain employees?

To motivate and retain employees:

Recognize their efforts, offer meaningful work, and provide training. A supportive culture helps keep employees happy.

16. What are standard operating procedures (SOPs)?

SOPs are detailed instructions for tasks to ensure consistency. Document steps, make them clear, and update as needed.

17. How do I manage my time effectively?

To manage your time effectively:

Prioritize tasks, plan your day, and delegate when possible. Use tools like calendars and task lists to stay organized.

18. What are KPIs in operations, and why are they important?

KPIs are metrics like delivery speed or customer satisfaction show how well operations are running. Tracking KPIs helps identify areas for improvement.

19. How do I handle seasonal fluctuations in demand?

To handle seasonal fluctuations in demand:

Adjust inventory, staffing, and marketing based on trends. Save cash during busy times to cover slower periods.

20. What are common operational challenges for small businesses, and how can I overcome them?

Challenges include limited resources and cash flow. Focus on priorities, track finances closely, and use automation to improve efficiency. Proactively addressing these challenges helps your business grow smoothly.

Chapter 10: Building and Managing a Team

1. When is the right time to hire my first employee?

Hire your first employee when your workload is too much to handle, when you need specific expertise, or when your focus shifts away from crucial tasks. Ensure your budget can support hiring.

2. What should I look for in potential team members?

In potential team members:

Seek candidates with relevant skills, adaptability, and a good cultural fit. Prioritize reliability, problem-solving, and a positive attitude.

3. How do I create a job description that attracts the right candidates?

Clearly outline the role, responsibilities, required skills, and company values. Include growth opportunities to attract motivated applicants.

4. Where can I find qualified candidates?

Job boards (LinkedIn, Indeed).
Networking events.
Employee referrals.
Social media.
University career centers.

5. How do I conduct effective interviews?

To conduct effective interviews:

Ask open-ended and situational questions to evaluate skills and cultural fit. Take notes and, if possible, involve another person for a second opinion.

6. How can I onboard new employees effectively?

To onboard new employees effectively:

Provide clear job instructions.
Introduce them to the team and culture.
Offer necessary tools and resources.
Schedule feedback sessions early on.

7. How do I create a positive workplace culture?

To create a positive workplace culture, build open communication, celebrate achievements, support work-life balance, and demonstrate mutual respect.

8. How can I motivate my team without a big budget?

To motivate your team without a big budget:

Recognize achievements, offer growth opportunities, and show genuine care for team members' goals. Small perks like flexible hours also help.

9. What are effective ways to manage remote teams?

To effectively manage remote teams:

Use tools like Trello or Asana, schedule regular check-ins, and ensure clear communication and accountability.

10. How do I establish clear roles and responsibilities?

To establish clear roles and responsibilities:

Use job descriptions and organizational charts. Regularly review and adapt roles as your business grows.

11. What is the best way to handle team conflicts?

The best way to handle team conflicts is to:

Address issues early with empathy. Listen to all sides, focus on solutions, and, if needed, involve a neutral mediator.

12. How do I set performance goals for my team?

To set performance goals for my team:

Use SMART criteria (Specific, Measurable, Achievable, Relevant, Time-bound). Align goals with business objectives and provide regular feedback.

13. What is the role of feedback in team management?

Feedback clarifies expectations, highlights strengths, and addresses weaknesses. Regular feedback promotes growth and alignment.

14. How can I delegate tasks effectively?

To delegate tasks effectively:

Match tasks to team members' strengths, provide clear instructions, and trust them to execute without micromanaging.

15. How do I retain talented employees?

To retain talented employees:

Offer a supportive culture, growth opportunities, and recognition. Provide competitive pay if possible and focus on work-life balance.

16. How do I handle underperformance?

To handle underperformance:

Address it promptly with specific feedback. Identify the cause, set improvement goals, and provide support like training.

17. How can I cultivate teamwork and collaboration?

To cultivate teamwork and collaboration:

Encourage open communication, use collaboration tools, assign team projects, and celebrate collective achievements.

18. What are employee development programs, and how do I create one?

Employee development programs are programs that focus on skill-building and career growth. Assess skill gaps, offer training, and provide mentorship opportunities.

19. How can I measure team performance?

To measure team performance:

Track KPIs like productivity, quality of work, goal completion, and engagement. Regular reviews help identify strengths and areas to improve.

20. How do I build trust and respect as a leader?

To build trust and respect as a leader:

Be transparent, treat everyone fairly, follow through on promises, and show appreciation for your team's efforts. Listen and act with integrity.

Chapter 11: Financial Basics for Entrepreneurs

1. What are the fundamentals of business finance?

The fundamentals of business finance are:

Managing money through budgeting, forecasting, and monitoring cash flow. This includes tracking income, expenses, assets, and liabilities to ensure profitability and stability.

2. How do I manage cash flow effectively?

To manage cash flow effectively:

Invoice promptly.
Monitor cash flow regularly.
Build a cash reserve for emergencies.

3. What are the key financial statements?

The key financial statements are:

Income Statement: Tracks revenue and expenses over time.
Balance Sheet: Shows assets, liabilities, and equity.
Cash Flow Statement: Tracks cash in and out of the business.

4. How can I keep expenses under control?

To keep expenses under control:

Create a budget, review spending regularly, and look for cost-saving opportunities like negotiating with suppliers.

5. What is a budget, and how do I create one?

A budget is a financial plan outlining income and expenses. Estimate revenue, list expenses, and compare actual spending to stay on track.

6. How do I set pricing to ensure profitability?

To set pricing to ensure profitability:

Factor in costs (COGS and operating expenses), desired profit margin, and competitor pricing. Ensure prices cover costs and provide profit.

7. What are fixed and variable costs?

Fixed Costs: Stay the same (e.g., rent).
Variable Costs: Change with production (e.g., materials).

Understanding these helps with pricing and planning.

8. How can I monitor profitability?

To monitor profitability:

Track gross and net profit margins and review financial statements to identify trends and opportunities for improvement.

9. What is break-even analysis?

Break-even analysis calculates when revenue will cover costs. Use it to set realistic sales targets and pricing.

10. How do I prepare for taxes?

To prepare for taxes:

Set aside money for taxes, keep detailed financial records, and understand deductions. Use accounting software or hire an accountant.

11. What are common tax deductions?

Common tax deductions include:

Home office expenses.
Business travel and meals.
Office supplies and equipment.
Marketing costs.

12. How do I build a cash reserve?

To build a cash reserve, save a portion of revenue consistently. Aim for 3–6 months of expenses to cover emergencies or slow periods.

13. What is business credit, and how do I establish it?

Business credit shows your financial reliability. Open a business bank account, use a credit card, and pay bills on time.

14. How do loans work, and when should I consider one?

Loans provide funds you repay with interest. Use them for growth or large expenses, ensuring you have a repayment plan.

15. What are accounts receivable and payable?

Accounts Receivable (AR): Money owed to you by customers.
Accounts Payable (AP): Money you owe to suppliers.

16. How can I improve cash flow?

To improve cash flow:

Offer discounts for early payments.
Reduce unnecessary expenses.
Avoid overstocking inventory.

17. What is financial forecasting?

Financial forecasting is predicting future revenue, expenses, and cash flow based on past data and market trends. It helps plan for growth and manage risks.

18. How do I make financial decisions?

To make financial decisions, base decisions on financial data, forecasts, and clear goals. Consider both short-term and long-term impacts.

19. How do I track and analyze financial performance?

To track and analyze financial performance:

Regularly review financial statements and KPIs like profit margin and revenue growth. Use accounting software to identify trends.

20. How can I prepare for financial challenges?

To prepare for financial challenges:

Build a cash reserve.
Diversify revenue streams.
Manage debt carefully.
Review expenses regularly.
Proactive planning and financial discipline can help your business stay resilient and adaptable.

Chapter 12: Legal and Regulatory Basics

1. What are the legal structures for businesses, and how do I choose one?

Common legal structures include:

Sole Proprietorship: Simple, but you're personally liable.
Partnership: Shared ownership, shared liability.
LLC: Limited liability, flexible taxes.
Corporation (C Corp, S Corp): Limited liability but more regulations.

Choose based on liability, taxes, and growth plans. Consult a lawyer or accountant.

2. Do I need a lawyer to start a business?

Not always, but a lawyer can help with contracts, IP, and compliance. Seek legal advice for complex issues or regulated industries.

3. What are the basic contracts I should know about?

The basic contracts you should know about are:

Operating Agreements (LLC roles and responsibilities).
Partnership Agreements.
NDAs (protect confidential info).
Employment Contracts.
Sales and Service Agreements.

4. How can I protect my intellectual property (IP)?

To protect your IP use:

Trademarks: For brand names and logos.
Patents: For inventions.
Copyrights: For creative works.
Trade Secrets: For proprietary processes.

5. What licenses and permits might I need?

The licenses and permits you need depends on your business and location.

Examples:

Business licenses.
Health and safety permits.
Professional licenses.
Zoning permits.

6. What is a registered agent, and do I need one?

A registered agent receives legal documents for your business. It's often required for LLCs and corporations.

7. How do I ensure compliance with industry regulations?

To ensure compliance with industry regulations:

Identify relevant rules (e.g., health, safety, data laws).
Create checklists and policies.
Conduct regular audits.

8. What is liability, and how can I protect my business?

Liability is legal responsibility for damages. You can protect your business by:

Choosing a structure like LLC or corporation.
Getting liability insurance.
Using contracts to clarify terms.

9. What types of insurance should I consider?

General Liability: Covers injury and property damage.
Professional Liability: Covers negligence claims.
Product Liability: Covers damages from your products.
Workers' Compensation: Required if you have employees.

10. What are employment laws, and how do they affect my business?

Employment laws cover hiring, pay, safety, and discrimination. Familiarity helps you create fair, compliant workplaces.

11. How can I protect my business in contracts?

To protect your business in contracts, use clear contracts detailing terms, pricing, deadlines, and dispute resolution. A legal review helps avoid risks.

12. What is data privacy, and how do I comply with laws?

Data privacy protects customer information. Compliance steps:
Adopt clear privacy policies.
Securely store data.
Follow laws like GDPR or CCPA.

13. How do I handle online terms of service and privacy policies?

To handle online terms of service and privacy policies:

Write clear terms explaining user rules and data practices. Update regularly to reflect changes in law or operations.

14. What is a business EIN, and do I need one?

A business EIN is a unique number for tax purposes. Needed for hiring employees, partnerships, and corporations.

15. What are trademarks, and how do I register one?

Trademarks protect your brand's name or logo. Register through the USPTO after ensuring originality.

16. How do I file taxes, and what should I know about deductions?

File taxes based on your business structure. Common deductions include rent, equipment, and travel. Keep detailed records.

17. What is a business succession plan?

A business succession is a plan for transferring ownership or management if you leave or can't continue. It ensures continuity and clarity for stakeholders.

18. What is a DBA, and when should I use one?

A DBA (Doing Business As) allows operating under a different name. Useful for branding or market expansion.

19. How do I avoid common legal pitfalls?

To avoid common legal pitfalls:

Choose the right structure.
Protect IP early.
Keep records for taxes and compliance.
Use contracts to formalize agreements.

20. When should I seek legal or regulatory help?

Seek help for complex tasks like forming partnerships, securing IP, or navigating employment laws. Regular legal check-ins ensure compliance.

Chapter 13: Risk Management and Problem Solving

1. What is risk management, and why is it important?

Risk management is the process of identifying, assessing, and mitigating threats to your business. Risk management helps minimize losses, protect your reputation, and ensure business continuity.

2. What are common types of risks businesses face?

Common types of risks businesses face are:

Financial (e.g., cash flow issues).
Operational (e.g., equipment failures).
Compliance (e.g., regulatory fines).
Reputational (e.g., negative publicity).
Cybersecurity (e.g., data breaches).

3. How do I identify risks in my business?

Analyze each area of your business, consider past challenges, and use tools like SWOT analysis to find vulnerabilities.

4. How do I conduct risk assessment?

To conduct risk assessment:

List potential risks, rate their likelihood and impact, and prioritize those with high likelihood and severe consequences. Develop strategies to mitigate them.

5. What is contingency planning, and why is it essential?

Contingency planning is preparing for unexpected disruptions. A contingency plan ensures quick responses to minimize downtime and maintain operations.

6. How can I create an effective contingency plan?

To create an effective contingency plan:

Identify crucial functions, potential risks, and backup solutions. Assign roles and test the plan regularly to ensure readiness.

7. What is business insurance, and how does it help?

Business insurance protects against risks like property damage, liability claims, or employee injuries. It transfers financial risk to the insurer, ensuring stability during disruptions.

8. How do I handle financial risk?

To handle financial risk:

Build cash reserves, monitor cash flow, diversify revenue streams, and review financial statements regularly.

9. What are cybersecurity risks, and how can I protect my business?

Cybersecurity risks include hacking and data breaches. Use strong passwords, update security software, train employees, and back up data regularly.

10. How can I minimize reputational risk?

To minimize reputational risk:

Provide excellent customer service, address complaints quickly, monitor social media, and maintain transparency in all dealings.

11. What are effective problem-solving techniques?

Effective problem-solving techniques include:

Root Cause Analysis: Find the main cause of an issue.
Brainstorming: Generate multiple solutions with your team.
5 Whys Technique: Keep asking "why" to uncover the root cause.

12. How can I involve my team in risk management and problem-solving?

To involve your team in risk management and problem-solving:

Encourage open communication, involve them in assessments, and brainstorm solutions. Their insights can highlight overlooked risks.

13. What is a crisis management plan, and when should I use it?

A crisis management plan is a detailed plan for urgent, high-impact events like natural disasters or data breaches. Use it for situations requiring coordinated, immediate responses.

14. How do I prioritize risks?

To prioritize risks:

Focus on risks with high likelihood and severe consequences first. Allocate resources efficiently to address the most critical threats.

15. How can I use data to solve problems?

To use data to solve problems:

Track metrics like sales or expenses to spot trends. Use analytics to identify issues and test solutions based on evidence.

16. How do I evaluate the effectiveness of a solution?

To evaluate the effectiveness of a solution:

Monitor KPIs, compare results to goals, and gather feedback. Adjust the solution if necessary for better results.

17. What is risk tolerance, and how do I determine mine?

Risk tolerance is how much risk your business can handle. Assess financial stability, industry volatility, and goals to decide your comfort level with risks.

18. How do I create a risk management policy?

To create a risk management policy:

Define objectives, outline procedures for assessing risks, assign responsibilities, and establish monitoring processes. A policy ensures consistent handling of risks.

19. How can I plan for supply chain disruptions?

To plan for supply chain disruptions:

Diversify suppliers, maintain safety stock, and build strong supplier relationships. Monitor trends to anticipate potential issues.

20. What is business resilience, and how can I build it?

Business resilience is the ability to adapt and recover from setbacks. You can build it by:

Creating contingency plans.
Encouraging team flexibility.
Maintaining strong relationships with customers and suppliers.
A resilient business is better equipped to thrive despite challenges.

Chapter 14: Scaling and Growing the Business

1. When is the right time to scale my business?

Scale when demand is steady, cash flow is stable, operations are reliable, and you have a clear plan for managing increased demand. Avoid scaling too early to prevent resource strain.

2. What's the difference between growth and scaling?

Growth adds revenue by increasing resources (e.g., hiring). Scaling increases revenue with minimal added costs by improving efficiency and automating processes.

3. How can I expand my customer base?

To expand your customer base:

Refine your marketing to target new audiences.
Use new sales channels like partnerships or online platforms.
Offer complementary products.
Encourage referrals through incentives.

4. How do I maintain quality and brand consistency as I grow?

To maintain quality and brand consistency as you grow:

Use a brand style guide and SOPs. Train your team, implement quality controls, and regularly review operations and customer feedback.

5. What are common challenges of scaling, and how can I overcome them?

Common challenges include cash flow, maintaining quality, and customer satisfaction. Overcome them by securing funding, using scalable technology, and focusing on customer service.

6. How can I attract investment or additional funding for growth?

To attract investment or additional funding for growth:

Show consistent revenue and customer acquisition.
Prepare a strong growth plan with clear financials.
Highlight your competitive advantage and scalability.
Target the right investors (e.g., VCs, banks, or angel investors).

7. What role does technology play in scaling?

Technology streamlines operations, automates tasks, and supports data-driven decisions. Use CRM systems, inventory management tools, and marketing automation for efficient growth.

8. How can I expand into new markets?

To expand into new markets:

Research new markets' needs, regulations, and competition. Adapt products and marketing to fit local preferences. Start small, test demand, and invest based on results.

9. What is customer segmentation, and how can it support growth?

Customer segmentation is dividing customers into segments based on demographics or behavior allows you to tailor marketing for better engagement and conversion rates.

10. How can I improve operational efficiency as I scale?

To improve operational efficiency as we scale, automate repetitive tasks, optimize workflows, and outsource non-core activities. Regularly review processes to eliminate bottlenecks.

11. How do I hire the right team for a growing business?

To hire the right team for a growing business:

Hire skilled, adaptable team members aligned with your culture. Define clear roles, provide thorough onboarding, and focus on people with a growth mindset.

12. How can I retain customers during scaling?

To retain customers during scaling:

Maintain consistent quality, offer loyalty programs, and prioritize personalized communication. Proactively address customer issues to preserve trust.

13. How do I set realistic growth goals?

To set realistic growth goals:

Use SMART goals (Specific, Measurable, Achievable, Relevant, Time-bound). Base them on market analysis, historical performance, and your business's capacity.

14. How do I manage cash flow during rapid growth?

To manage cash flow during rapid growth:

Negotiate longer payment terms with suppliers.
Offer discounts for early receivables payments.
Maintain a cash reserve for unexpected costs.

15. How do I balance growth with quality control?

To balance growth with quality control:

Implement quality checks, train staff, and use tools to monitor metrics. SOPs and customer feedback loops help maintain high standards.

16. What are economies of scale, and how can my business benefit?

Economies of scale reduce the cost per unit as production increases. Negotiate bulk discounts, streamline processes, and leverage technology to lower costs.

17. How can I manage increased customer service demands?

To manage increased customer service demands:

Scale customer service with helpdesk software, chatbots, and a trained support team. Offer self-service options like FAQs and knowledge bases.

18. How can partnerships support growth?

Partnering with complementary businesses or influencers expands your reach, shares resources, and opens new revenue opportunities.

19. What is a growth strategy, and how do I create one?

A growth strategy outlines steps for expansion. Define goals, assess capacity, and plan tactics like entering new markets or increasing product offerings.

20. How can I measure the success of my scaling efforts?

To measure the success of your scaling efforts, monitor metrics like:

Revenue Growth: Increased sales over time.
Customer Retention Rates: Loyal customers staying engaged.
Profit Margins: Ensuring profitability improves with growth.
Operational Efficiency: Productivity and cost savings.
Review these regularly to adjust strategies and ensure alignment with your goals.

Chapter 15: Exit Strategies and Future Planning

1. What is an exit strategy, and why do I need one?

An exit strategy is a plan for how you will eventually leave or transfer ownership of your business. It allows you to maximize the value of your business, ensure a smooth transition, and achieve personal and financial goals. Planning ahead prepares you for both voluntary and involuntary exits, such as retirement or unexpected life changes.

2. What are the most common exit strategies for small businesses?

The most common exit strategies include:

Selling the Business: Transferring ownership to a buyer in exchange for cash or equity.
Merger or Acquisition: Combining with or being acquired by another company for strategic growth.
Family Succession: Passing the business to a family member as part of a legacy plan.
Management Buyout (MBO): Selling the business to your management team or employees.
Going Public (IPO): Offering shares on the stock market, ideal for high-growth businesses.
Liquidation: Selling off assets and closing the business, often as a last resort.

3. How do I determine the best exit strategy for my business?

To determine the best exit strategy for my business:

Consider your personal goals, financial needs, and vision for the business. Assess factors like market value, desired involvement post-exit, and potential buyers. A financial advisor or business consultant can help identify the most suitable strategy.

4. How can I prepare my business for sale?

To prepare your business for sale:

Organize financial records and ensure accuracy.
Optimize operations by streamlining processes and documenting SOPs.
Build a loyal customer base with steady revenue.
Increase profitability and demonstrate positive cash flow.
Resolve any legal or compliance issues.

5. What are business valuation methods?

Business valuation methods include:

Asset-Based Valuation: Evaluating total assets minus liabilities.
Earnings Multiples: Applying a multiple to annual revenue or profit.
Discounted Cash Flow (DCF): Estimating future cash flow discounted to present value.
Hiring a professional appraiser ensures accuracy and facilitates fair negotiations.

6. What is a succession plan, and when should I create one?

A succession plan outlines how ownership and leadership will transition. It's ideal to create one several years in advance to allow time for training successors and ensuring continuity. This minimizes disruptions and prepares the business for a seamless transfer.

7. How can I ensure a smooth transition for new owners or management?

To ensure a smooth transition for new owners or management, provide:

Comprehensive documentation, including SOPs, financial records, and customer data.

Training for new owners or management.
Transparent communication with employees, customers, and suppliers.
Availability for consultation during the transition period.

8. What are the tax implications of selling a business?

Selling a business may involve capital gains taxes, which vary depending on the sale structure (asset sale vs. stock sale). Certain deductions, like goodwill or retirement contributions, may reduce tax liability. Consult a tax advisor to optimize tax outcomes.

9. How do I negotiate the sale of my business?

Here are some steps to negotiate the sale of my business:

Understanding your business's value.
Defining your goals for the sale (e.g., price, post-sale involvement).
Being open to different payment structures (e.g., lump sum, installments).
Using a broker or negotiator to manage complex terms and secure favorable agreements.

10. How does a merger or acquisition (M&A) work?

M&A involves combining with or being acquired by another company. Key steps include:

Valuing your business and assessing strategic fit.
Negotiating terms of the deal, including payment and leadership roles.
Legal and financial due diligence to ensure smooth integration.
M&As can provide growth opportunities and increased resources.

11. How can I pass my business to a family member?

To pass my business to a family member, steps include:

Involving the successor early in business operations.
Providing formal training and leadership development.
Creating a clear legal and financial transfer plan.
Family succession allows for preserving legacy but requires planning to avoid conflicts.

12. What is an Employee Stock Ownership Plan (ESOP)?

An ESOP enables employees to acquire shares in the business over time. It serves as a succession plan, improves employee motivation, and ensures continuity. Consult experts to structure an ESOP that aligns with your goals.

13. What are the pros and cons of liquidating a business?

Pros: Quick access to cash, no ongoing obligations.
Cons: Potential loss of value, possible reputational impact, and unmet obligations to stakeholders.

Liquidation is often a last resort and works best for businesses without significant goodwill.

14. How can I maintain business value as I plan for an exit?

To maintain business value as you plan for an exit:

Maintain quality, customer satisfaction, and operational efficiency. Keep financial records up to date, reduce unnecessary expenses, and avoid major disruptions. Consistency ensures maximum value at the time of exit.

15. What should I communicate to employees during an exit?

To communicate to employees during an exit:

Inform employees early, focusing on how the transition affects their roles. Provide reassurances about job security and the company's future. Transparent communication builds trust and minimizes uncertainty.

16. How can I manage emotional aspects of exiting a business?

To manage the emotional aspects of exiting a business:

Reflect on the reasons for your exit and focus on future opportunities. Seek support from mentors, family, or a business coach to process emotions. Acknowledge the significance of your achievements and plan for a fulfilling next chapter.

17. What is legacy planning, and how can I build a lasting legacy?

Legacy planning shapes the long-term impact of your business.

Focus on:

Establishing a strong company culture.
Supporting community initiatives or causes.
Documenting your business's story and values.
A well-planned legacy enhances reputation and creates lasting value.

18. How do I ensure ongoing income after selling or exiting my business?

To ensure ongoing income after selling or exiting my business, options include:

Negotiating a gradual buyout or retaining a minority stake.
Setting up royalties or licensing agreements.
Investing sale proceeds into income-generating assets
Proper planning ensures financial stability post-exit.

19. How can I use my business exit to support future endeavors?

Leverage your experience, reputation, and proceeds to:

Invest in new ventures.
Mentor or consult other entrepreneurs.
Contribute to community or industry initiatives.
Your exit can serve as a launchpad for new opportunities.

20. How can I start planning for an exit early in my business journey?

To start planning for an exit early in your business journey:

Include exit planning in your initial business plan. Regularly update financial records, streamline operations, and build a reliable team. Early planning provides flexibility and ensures you're prepared for a successful exit whenever the time comes.

Chapter 16: Entrepreneurial Mindset and Continuous Learning

1. What is an entrepreneurial mindset?

An entrepreneurial mindset is a way of thinking that helps you stay creative, adaptable, and ready to handle challenges in business.

2. Why is it important to have an entrepreneurial mindset?

It is important to have an entrepreneurial mindset because it helps you deal your problems, stay motivated, and keep improving your business.

3. How can I stay strong when things go wrong?

To stay strong when things go wrong, take care of yourself, set small goals, and learn from mistakes. Talking to mentors or friends can also help.

4. Why is being flexible important for business?

Being flexible is important for business because it helps you adjust when things change, like customer needs or market trends, so your business keeps moving forward.

5. How do I stay motivated as an entrepreneur?

To stay motivated as an entrepreneur:

Set goals, celebrate wins, and do things you enjoy outside of work. Remember why you started your business.

6. What can I learn from failure?

To learn from failure:

Look at what went wrong and think about how you can do better next time. Mistakes can teach you a lot.

7. Why is learning new things important for my business?

Learning new things is important for your business because it helps you keep up with changes, improve your skills, and make smarter decisions.

8. How can I keep learning as a business owner?

To keep learning as a business owner:

Read books, take courses, listen to podcasts, and attend workshops or events.

9. How do I come up with new ideas for my business?

To come up with new ideas for my business:

Listen to feedback, try new things, and keep an open mind. Pay attention to trends in your industry.

10. How can I get better at solving problems?

To get better at solving problems:

Break the problem into smaller parts and think of different ways to fix it. Practice helps you get better.

11. Why is curiosity good for business?

Curiosity helps you ask questions, look for new ideas, and find better ways to do things.

12. How can I meet helpful people in business?

To meet helpful people in business:

Join events, online groups, or local business networks. Talk to people who have experience in your field.

13. Why is self-discipline important?

Self-discipline is important because it keeps you focused, helps you manage time, and ensures you get things done even when it's hard.

14. How can I balance work and personal life?

To balance work and personal life balance:

Set clear work hours, take breaks, and make time for family, friends, and hobbies.

15. How do I set goals that I can achieve?

Make goals specific and realistic. Break big goals into smaller steps so they're easier to work on.

16. How can I help my team stay positive and learn new things?

Encourage your team to try new skills, support them when they make mistakes, and recognize their efforts.

17. How do I stay positive during tough times?

To stay positive during tough times, focus on what's going well, think about solutions instead of problems, and spend time with supportive people.

18. How can I plan for the future of my business?

To plan for the future of your business, think about where you want your business to be in five or ten years and what steps you need to take to get there.

19. Why should I work on understanding emotions?

Working on understanding emotions helps you communicate better, handle stress, and build good relationships with your team and customers.

20. What kind of legacy do I want to leave as an entrepreneur?

Think about how you want people to remember you, whether it's through the values you stood for, the people you helped, or the impact your business made.

Conclusion

Congratulations on completing this guide to entrepreneurship! You've studied the basics of starting, managing, and growing a business. With what you've learned about research, finances, branding, and building the right mindset, you're ready to make thoughtful decisions and move forward confidently.

Start small, but always keep your bigger goals in mind. Growth takes time, so focus on steady progress and celebrate each milestone along the way. Challenges are part of the process, so stay open to learning and adapting as you go. Your customers are at the heart of your business. Understand their needs, build strong relationships, and create great experiences. A happy customer is more likely to stick with you and recommend your business.

The entrepreneurial journey has its ups and downs, but resilience and determination will help you overcome obstacles. Every challenge is an opportunity to learn and grow stronger. Planning gives you direction, but action drives progress. Take consistent steps every day, and those efforts will lead to meaningful results over time. As you apply these ideas and build your vision, trust yourself and remember why you started. Your passion, determination, and creativity make your business unique. With each step, you're moving closer to creating something impactful and rewarding.

Thank you for taking the time to invest in yourself and your goals through this guide. The skills and insights you've gained will help you create something truly special. Celebrate your progress, enjoy the process, and take pride in every success.

www.ingramcontent.com/pod-product-compliance
Lightning Source LLC
Chambersburg PA
CBHW071110240526
45469CB00006BD/2412